W9-API-773

James W. Moore

JESUS'

Parables About
Discipleship

ABINGDON PRESS

NASHVILLE

JESUS' PARABLES ABOUT DISCIPLESHIP

Copyright © 2009 by Abingdon Press

This book is printed on acid-free paper.

Library of Congress Cataloging-in-Publication Data

Moore, James W. (James Wendell), 1938–
    Jesus' parables about discipleship / James W. Moore.
        p.   cm.
    ISBN 978-0-687-64695-1 (binding: pbk., adhesive, perfect : alk. paper)
1. Jesus Christ—Parables.   2. Christian life—Methodist authors.   I. Title.

BT375.3.M64   2009
226.8—dc22

                                                                2008052934

10 11 12 13 14 15 16 17 18—10 9 8 7 6 5 4 3

MANUFACTURED IN THE UNITED STATES OF AMERICA

For Sarah, Paul, Dawson, Daniel, and Mason

CONTENTS

INTRODUCTION

Why did Jesus use parables, and how do we unravel them and discover their timeless and powerful messages? Let me begin by giving you five key ideas that help unlock the truths found in all the parables of Jesus.

First, Jesus spoke in parables—short stories that teach a faith lesson—to be understood and remembered, to proclaim the good news, and to make people think.

Second, Jesus saw himself as one who came to serve the needy, and he believed that the kingdom of God existed anywhere kingdom-deeds such as love, mercy, kindness, and compassion were being done.

Third, God's love for us is unconditional; and God

wants us to love one another in the same way—unconditionally.

Fourth, one way to discover the central truth of a parable is to look for the surprise in it. Look for the moment when you lift your eyebrows, or the moment when the original hearers of the story probably thought or said in surprise—or maybe even shock—"Oh, my goodness, did you hear that?"

Fifth, it's important to remember that parables are designed to convey one central truth. Parables (as opposed to allegories, in which everything in the story has a symbolic meaning) make one main point.

Parables slip up on us. They flip our values. They turn our world upside down. They surprise us. This is the great thing about the parables of Jesus: they are always relevant and always personal. They speak eloquently to you and me, here and now. In this book, we will examine some of Jesus' thought-provoking parables about discipleship to see if we can find ourselves, and God's truth for us, in these magnificent truth-stories. They are, after all, truth-stories for us—truth-stories from the mind of Jesus that can change our lives as they proclaim God's truth for you and me.

1

Unconditional Love
"What Is the Good News?"

Scripture: Luke 15:11-24

Let me begin by stringing together three short stories. The thread that links them together will be obvious.

First, one father said that he had noticed something fascinating about children, namely, that as they develop and grow they pass through some predictable stages, and these stages are characterized by the way they address their fathers. He said that they begin by calling you "Da Da," then they call you "Daddy," next they call you "Dad," and then they call you *collect*!

The second story is about a little five-year-old boy who got on his mother's nerves one afternoon. He upset his mother so much that in frustration she grabbed the broom and chased after him. The boy ran into the yard and scrambled under the house. Unable to reach him and unwilling to go under the house, the mother decided to let Dad deal with the five-year-old when he got home.

A short time later, the father arrived home, heard the story, and went under the house in search of the little boy. Crawling on his hands and knees, searching with a flashlight, he quickly found him.

When the little boy saw his father, he said it as only a five-year-old little boy could, "Hi, Dad. Is she after you, too?"

Now, the third story is found in the Bible. In Luke's Gospel we discover a magnificent story about a father, which has been called, fittingly, the greatest short story ever written. Even though we usually call it the parable of the prodigal son, this story is really about the father. The key message here is not found in the revelry of the prodigal son; nor is it found in the resentful self-righteousness of the elder brother. No, the real truth Jesus wanted to communicate here is dramatically wrapped up in this loving, gracious, forgiving father; and the greatness of the parable is that here in this story, in this father, we have the picture of God as Jesus saw God and understood him and imaged him.

Don't miss this now: in this parable, Jesus is painting his portrait of God. And notice how Jesus depicts God not as a stern, unbending taskmaster; not as an angry judge demanding his pound of flesh; but as a loving parent, as a father who is kind and compassionate and merciful, as a father who genuinely cares for all of his children with all of his heart.

Look at the story. The prodigal does everything wrong at first, demands his inheritance early, runs away from home, and squanders his money in the far country, living it up. But then, he comes to his senses and returns home, ashamed, penitent, sorry for the pain he has caused, feeling unworthy and humble, rehearsing the confession he has carefully prepared.

Now, as he walks down the road toward home, his father sees him. The father has been looking down that road a hundred times every day, hoping and praying for this moment, hoping and praying that his son would come home. And, at long last, there he is. The father explodes with joy at the sight of him. And the father runs to meet his son. The father runs toward him to greet him, to welcome him, to reassure him with thanksgiving on his lips, with love in his heart, and with the tears of happy relief in his eyes. The father hugs his son tightly, calls for a great celebration, and with bigness of spirit he brings the prodigal back into the family circle. Isn't that a great story? With good reason, it has been called the greatest short story of all time.

Some years ago when I was in college, I had a classmate named Jack. Jack was a real character: if I made a list of the most unusual characters I have ever met, Jack would easily be in the top ten. He always wore a black suit, a white shirt, and a solid black tie, and rain or shine, Jack always carried a large black umbrella. He was of German descent and proud of it. Sometimes he would speak to me in German, sometimes in English, and sometimes he would try to speak in a southern drawl, which he butchered terribly. He was not making fun when he tried the southern drawl; he thought it made me more comfortable. Jack was a rare and wonderful character.

And he was the talk of the campus not for his eccentric ways, however, but because in our first year of college Jack had not worked out his theology yet; and he had, like the great Protestant reformer Martin Luther (whom Jack so much admired), a troubled soul. Jack, like Luther in his early years, had a bad image of God. Like Luther, Jack was scared to death of God. He was terrified of God, and this fear of God reflected itself most graphically in Jack's attitude toward the altar. The altar table in the college chapel was quite simple, actually—just a white table with a cross and two candles on it—but it struck fear in Jack's heart because it represented for him the presence of God, and he was scared of God. We had chapel every day, and every day the students would rush to chapel to see how Jack would "handle the altar today."

Some days, Jack would stand in the back of the chapel with his head bowed, and he would pray silently. Some days, he would walk all the way up to the altar and kneel before it, or he might fall down on all fours before it. Some days, he would stand and look at the altar in deep meditation. And other days, he would drop on one knee and make the sign of the cross.

And when we had Communion, Jack would always slip up to the altar after the service and eat all of the leftovers, because they had been consecrated, and he felt that to consecrate the elements and then not use all of them would somehow make God angry.

Once in preaching class Jack accidentally walked between the altar and the congregation. Horrified, he grabbed his head, turned, and did a deep Shakespearean bow. Then he rushed to the pulpit and stammered out an apology. Unable to preach, he ran out of the chapel with tears in his eyes. Jack was frustrated and ill at ease and confused, and he later admitted that his confusion came from his awful fear of God.

Everything Jack did, he did to try to win God's love, to appease God, to get God to forgive him and accept him, until a wise professor did a very wise thing. The professor asked Jack to write a paper on Jesus' parable of the prodigal son. As he studied those words of Jesus, Jack discovered something that set him free and changed his life.

Jack discovered through the mind of Jesus and the words of Jesus that he didn't have to win God's love; he already had it. God had loved him all along. In that parable, Jesus paints God's picture, and he paints God boldly and tenderly as a loving father; not as an austere, impersonal, hostile God who is out to get us, but as a loving father who runs down the road to meet us, and who celebrates our homecoming because he cares for us and has goodwill for us. Jack discovered through studying the Scriptures that God loves us, that God is on our side, that God is a caring Father.

That is the good news of our faith: God is like a forgiving, loving parent, like the father in the story. There is so much to learn from him. Let me show you what I mean.

First, the Father in the Parable Is the Example of Patience

The father lets his son test his wings and patiently waits, even though it is painful. Harold Wilke was an incredible person, a spellbinding speaker, and a noted author. His achievements were all the more remarkable because Mr. Wilke was born without arms and hands. He had learned to do everything with his feet and toes. Using this method, he could drive a car, take his glasses on and off, write books, and sign autographs. "How did you learn to do that?" a TV host once asked. In answer, Harold Wilke told of a childhood experience that stuck in his mind because it tells the story so well.

It was a hot summer day. Harold Wilke was a small child at the time and he was sitting on the floor trying to take off a T-shirt. He was having a difficult time. Can you imagine trying to take off a T-shirt, on a hot, muggy day, using your feet and your toes? It was frustrating and agonizing. A neighbor was visiting in the family's home, and she saw little Harold's difficulty and said to Harold's mother, "Why don't you help that child?" His mother replied: "I am helping him." The patience of Harold Wilke's mother paid off, because he became an inspiration to millions (Wilke, *Using Everything You've Got* [National Easter Seal Society, 1984], 25).

That's the kind of patience the father in the parable had. It's God's kind of patience. It's the kind of patience we all need.

Second, the Father in the Parable Is the Example of Forgiveness

The father in Jesus' parable doesn't demand an apology. He doesn't say, "I told you so." He doesn't write a list of conditions. He just runs down the road to meet his child with the spirit of forgiveness in his heart.

Just this week I ran across an old legend about Satan calling a staff meeting in hell. He calls together his leading evil executives to map out a strategy against the church. Satan tells them to urge people to be jealous and resentful, to encourage them to be harsh and unbending, to teach them to be hateful and judgmental. "And whatever you do," says Satan, "try to stamp out the spirit of forgiveness, because if Christians ever realize the power of forgiveness and compassion, then hell help us, because all heaven's gonna break loose."

This parable is about a forgiving father, but sadly, as we read further we see it is also about an unforgiving son (Luke 15:25-32). The elder brother is bitter and envious and angry, and he will not forgive, and that attitude makes him miss the party. The point is that God is forgiving and God wants us to be forgiving, too.

Finally, the Father in the Parable Is the Example of Love— *Agape*, Unconditional Love

Have you heard about the young man who was drafted into the army? Immediately he seemed to have psychological problems. He began to do a bizarre thing. Every time he saw a piece of paper, he would run and pick it up, look at it, and say, "That's not it. That's not it," and then the young man would put the paper down.

He did this over and over, every day. He was obsessed with it. Finally, the young man was sent to the base psychiatrist. The psychiatrist worked with the young man, but he continued to look at every piece of paper he saw and say, "That's not it. That's not it." When the psychiatrist asked him why he was doing this, he answered, "I'm looking for something." When asked what he was looking for, he replied, "I'll know it when I see it."

The psychiatrist could get nowhere with this patient, so finally army officials called the young man in and explained to him that under the circumstances, he could not stay in the army, and so they gave him his discharge paper. The young man took the discharge paper in his hand, he looked at it, smiled, and said: "That's *it*! That's *it*!"

Now, something like that happened to me in my search for God. I read lots of different ideas and descriptions of what God is like: "The First Cause," "The Unmoved Mover," "The Progenitor," "The Awesome Judge"; but none of them grabbed me, and I would put down what I was reading and say, "That's not it for me." But then I came upon the parable of the prodigal son. The parable is great in and of itself, but what makes it even greater is the One who told it. When I read that, those powerful words of Jesus, and saw how he pictured God as a loving Father, I said, "That's *it*! That's *it*!"

Here, Jesus shows us what God is like and what God wants us to be like, and the word is *love*. That's it! That's the gospel! That's the good news!

2
Humility
"Presumptuous Religion"

Scripture: Luke 14:7-11

All of us have deep down within us what Wallace Hamilton called "the drum major instinct." That is, we all want to excel, we all want to achieve success, we all want to be recognized for our performance, we all want to accomplish something meaningful and worthwhile, or in other words, we all want to lead the parade. Or as Carl Sandburg put it, we "all want to play Hamlet."

Alfred Adler, one of the fathers of modern psychiatry, described it as the dominant impulse in human nature. He said this desire for recognition, this wish to be somebody, this yearning to be significant, is our strongest emotion. I don't know if Adler is right about that, but I think we would all agree that the drum major instinct is a basic and important part of our human makeup.

However, we have to watch it; it can get out of hand; it can be taken too far. We have to be very careful with this assertive drive, or it may become a monstrous, ruthless tyrant. It may become an arrogant, presumptuous attitude that pushes and shoves and elbows other people out of the way.

To be presumptuous is to be arrogantly proud or overly bold. It is to take undue liberties. It is the opposite of humility. Sometimes people are presumptuous in their interpersonal relationships, being haughty, egotistical, and unappreciative, and taking others for granted.

I remember the first time I really understood the word *presumptuous*. I was a freshman in college, living in Epworth Hall on the Lambuth College campus in Jackson, Tennessee. I was there on scholarship, playing basketball for the Lambuth Eagles. I came in from basketball practice one evening; my roommate met me at the door, telling me not to be upset. An upperclassman named Marty from down the hall had come into our room, had gone through my desk, had found my car keys, and had borrowed my car without asking.

I had worked two jobs all summer to save enough money to buy that car, a shiny black 1950 Ford. It was a used car, but it was my prize possession. Not only that, but Marty also had gone through my closet, picking out and putting on my nicest and newest shirt, one I had never worn because I was saving it for a special occasion. He left, driving my new car and wearing my new shirt.

Now, if that weren't presumptuous enough, wait until you hear, as Paul Harvey would put it, "the rest of the story." When Marty returned at midnight, I immediately noticed that he had spilled a chocolate milkshake on my shirt. As he handed me the car keys, he told me that my car was on Highland Street, two miles away; he had run out of gas. He suggested that I should keep more gas in my car.

Now, that's a dramatic example of a presumptuous attitude, and it is not a very pretty picture, is it? I have been thinking recently that it is also possible to be presumptuous in religion. This kind of presumptuous religion was expressed recently by a well-known show-business personality whose name you would recognize. This person said, "I believe in God, but I don't like the organized church. A man can get as much religion down on his knees in his own home. When I get to heaven Jesus will be the kind of guy I want him to be! He's going to go golfing with me every day, and if he doesn't like to golf, then Jesus can caddy for me!" That is presumptuous religion! The presumptuous attitudes of people are bothersome, aren't they?

The presumptuous attitudes of people must have bothered Jesus greatly, because one of his most famous parables and one of his most haunting sayings dealt with this kind of haughtiness. And Jesus suggested that presumptuous people are brought down by their own presumptuous attitudes.

Remember the scene: Jesus was the invited guest of honor in the home of a wealthy Pharisee. Other prominent persons were present as well—lawyers, teachers of the Law, high-ranking officials. Jesus had noticed earlier with quiet amusement and sad dismay the sly, scheming ways in which the leaders worked and manipulated to promote themselves.

He had noticed how they loved to take the chief seats in the synagogue and the high places of prominence at public functions. What Jesus had noticed before was repeated here.

When the guests were called to dinner there was an ugly, unseemly rush toward the tables, not so much for the best food, but for position at the table. The rush was for the best seats, the places of prominence.

In Eastern lands, hospitality was regarded as the most prized social virtue; the Talmud set down clear rules for its procedure. Protocol—who sits where, and in what precise order—was of major importance in etiquette. The rule was that the uppermost seat was reserved for the most worthy guest. He sat on the left, the next most worthy on the right, with the host in between, and so on, down to the last and least worthy. This often made for embarrassing situations.

It did here in Jesus' parable. When the scramble for seats was over and the dust cleared, the host was embarrassed to discover that his main guest of honor had apparently lost out in the scramble. Instead of being in the chief seat, the guest of honor had taken the last seat, the lowest place, while a self-important person was complacently occupying the seat of honor. There followed a moment of awkward silence when the host had to rearrange the seating.

The presumptuous man was called down. The presumptuous man, now red-faced, had to step down in front of everybody, while the modest man who had refused to push and shove and elbow was called higher: "Excuse me, my friend; you are the guest of honor. Come higher. This is the place I have for you. You belong here." So simple an occurrence, yet Jesus used it as a parable of eternal truth.

The humble attitude beats the presumptuous attitude every time. The humble spirit is so much better, so much more Christlike, than the arrogant, pushy, presumptuous spirit.

There is a warning here for all of us—namely, beware of being presumptuous; but even more, beware of presumptuous religion! Let me illustrate this further by listing some tricky, presumptuous attitudes that we need to be wary of in our faith pilgrimage.

Beware of Presuming That We Have All the Answers

Beware of becoming arrogantly closed-minded. Beware of presumptuously thinking that "my way is the only way." You see, we must keep on growing, stretching, learning. We must be humbly open to new truths from God.

On a recent trip to New York, I discovered my cab driver was from Honolulu. I asked him how to correctly pronounce the name of his state: "Is it Ha-*wa*-ii, or Ha-*va*-ii?" He said, "Ha-*va*-ii." I said thank you, and he said, "You're *vel*come!" Even when we think we have the answer, some new truth can give it a different slant. We must be open to new insights and new ideas.

How presumptuous it is to imagine that we have all the answers regarding God's magnificent and mysterious universe. It's like going down to the ocean and saying, "I can put it all in my pocket." God's universe is filled with mystery, and it is the height of haughtiness to close the book on truth.

That's what Jim Jones tried to do. He tried to close the book on truth. He thought he had all the answers. He thought he was the only truth, and anyone who differed with him or even questioned him was punished cruelly; and that kind of closed-mindedness led to the Guyana tragedy.

A call to discipleship is a call to grow in the faith. The word *disciple* means "learner," one who is learning the faith. Good, healthy faith is humble faith that keeps on growing. It is not content with one experience with God or a few simplistic religious notions. Many people who fall away from the faith do so because they stop growing. When we stop growing spiritually, we begin to die spiritually.

Remember the story about the little boy who fell out of bed one night. His father rushed in to check on him and said, "What happened, son?" The boy answered, "I don't know, Dad; I guess I just fell asleep too close to where I got in!"

This can happen to us in our spiritual lives, can't it? Presumptuously thinking we have all the answers, we get lazy, and we fall asleep too close to where we got in.

When I first got out of seminary, I went through a rather presumptuous period that I am ashamed to think of now. When I thought I was supposed to be some kind of "super preacher," a man with all the answers, I learned through the hard knocks of life that we are justified, not by simplistic, sanctimonious answers, but rather by faith and a loving, gracious, merciful, compassionate, forgiving God.

That early experience, however, made me identify personally with something that happened to a young minister. David, too, came out of seminary ready to solve all the problems of the world single-handedly. He had been trained, he had studied hard, he had been a good student, and now, as a pastor in a little community in Virginia, he was ready to lay religion on the people. He was ready to give his answers with a pious, religious, authoritative tone. David thought he had all the answers, thought he was in complete control, thought he was "the answer man," as the months passed quickly by.

One day the telephone rang in his study. The father of a board chairman of the church suddenly had died. As David started to the family's home, it suddenly hit him: *I don't know what to say. I'm their pastor, and I'm scared.* David tried to recall appropriate Scripture passages to quote. He tried to think of some theological message to give these people in their shocked hour of need. He plotted his strategy: "I'll go in, gather all the family in the living room, and quote the Twenty-third Psalm. That's what I'll do; that's the answer!" But there was something David hadn't counted on. When he got to the home and had gathered the family in the living room, as he looked across those mournful faces, he realized for the first time how much he loved these people. His heart broke along with them; he was overcome with emotion. He loved these people, and their hurt was his hurt; and as he opened his mouth to say the Twenty-third Psalm, no words would come, only sobs. David burst into tears, and he cried his eyes out. So much so, that the family had to come over to minister to him. David was so embarrassed, so ashamed. He felt that he had failed his people in their hour of need.

Shortly after, David was transferred to another church. Fifteen years or so passed. One day, David ran into that board chairman. David winced as he remembered that day, but then something happened that surprised him. The man's face lit up, he ran to David and hugged him tightly, and he said, "Oh, David, I'm so glad to see you! Our family loves and appreciates you so much. We miss you! We talk about you all the time. We'll never forget the time when Daddy died, how you came and cried with us!" David couldn't give answers that day, but unknowingly he had given that family something better: he had given them his love.

We need to beware of presuming that we have all the answers.

Beware of Presuming That God Should Bless Us at the Expense of Others

A number of religious magazines come across my desk. Some of them I have ordered, while others just appear. Recently I came across an article titled "How God Answered My Prayer." It was the testimony of a businessman. He and a coworker were up for a promotion, and both were being considered for a prestigious position with the company. The man said he really wanted that job, so he prayed about it. Just before the selection was made, the other man had a heart attack and was hospitalized, and he was taken out of consideration; so, the man writing the article said, "I got the job. That's how God answered my prayer."

How presumptuous! To imagine that God would give one of his children a heart attack in order to answer the prayer of another of his children. We must be very careful in our prayer life that we are not presumptuous, that we don't ask God to bless us at the expense of others.

Beware of Presuming That People Know We Love Them and Appreciate Them

In *Fiddler on the Roof*, there is a poignant scene where Tevye, the main character, keeps asking his wife, "Do you love me?" She keeps brushing the question aside by talking of how she has lived with him for so many years. Yet Tevye persists: "But do you love me?" His wife, Golde, talks about how she has worked side by side with him and kept the house. Again Tevye asks, "But do you love me?" Again Golde sidesteps the question by reminding him of how she has borne his children and reared them. But Tevye is not satisfied. He sees his daughters growing up, courting, marrying, and now suddenly the feeling of love runs strong within him. He wants to hear it; he needs to hear it. He wants his wife to say it out loud. He needs reassurance; he wants to know that it is still the same with them. He needs to hear the words *I love you.*

It's presumptuous of us to assume that people know we love them and appreciate them, and never tell them. Husband and wife live together day-in and day-out; surely they love one another, but has it been said lately? Father and son, mother and daughter, sister and brother, living together under the same roof; surely they love one another, but how long has it been since it was said?

Christian friends live next to one another, serve in the same church, share the same pew, sing in the same choir, study in the same Sunday school class. Surely they love one another, but has it been said? Has it been expressed? Has it been verbalized?

Neighbors across a backyard fence, partners across an office desk; we presume our friends know that we love them and appreciate them, but still the question rings out: Has it been said? Have we told them? Have we told them lately?

I confess to you, I am guilty here. There are literally hundreds of letters I need to write, hundreds of phone calls I need to make, hundreds of "thank yous" I need to express, hundreds of "I love yous" that I need to verbalize. May God forgive us at this point?

Every now and then, I think of William Sangster's story about writing letters of gratitude to people who had touched his life in special ways. One went to a former schoolteacher. Her answer to him is haunting: "Dear Willie, Your letter came on a wet, cold, and lonely day. I am retired now and living alone. Your words brightened my day. I taught school for nearly fifty years, and I want you to know that yours was the first thank-you letter I ever received."

To fail to express love and gratitude to others is to be presumptuous, and how guilty most of us are at this point.

Beware of Presuming That Someone Else Will Uphold the Church

Some people want a good church, but they want somebody else to see to it! Some people want a good choir, but they want someone else to do the singing. Some want a good Sunday school, but they expect somebody else to see to it. Some want a good youth program, but they want someone else to cook those hot dogs and climb onto the hayride truck.

What if every member of our church were exactly like you; what kind of church would we have? What if every member came to church as often, or as seldom, as you come? What if every member gave what you give, served as you serve? What kind of church would we have? That's worth thinking about, because we must beware of presuming that someone else will uphold the church.

Beware of Presuming That Our Wants Are More Important than God's Will

Sometimes what we want and what God wants happen to be the same thing. Oftentimes they are not. We need to be open to that. Remember Jesus in the garden of Gethsemane, praying. He didn't want to go to the cross. He didn't choose that. He said, "Father, let this cup pass from me. Not my will, but thine be done."

Thy will be done! In that classic scene, we have the graphic picture of humility, and it's the opposite of presumptuous religion.

3

Service
"You Want Me to Play Second String?"

Scripture: Matthew 25:14-30

One of the most painful experiences in life is that moment when you realize that you are not quite good enough, not quite tall enough, not quite fast enough, not quite talented enough to make the first team. You try out for the team; you give your all; you have great dreams of being a star. But then gradually you begin to realize that others are inching ahead of you, and ultimately you are relegated to the second team, the "B" team, the scrubs, the reserves. Oh how that hurts, oh, the pain of that, what a disappointment.

It's tough to be a second stringer. You have to make every practice. You have to work as hard as anyone, knowing that you might not even get in the game, knowing that you likely will never make headlines or be in the star-studded limelight, because you are a second stringer. Some people have a hard time handling that. Some quit the team. They refuse to accept that role. Unable to live with being second string, they get angry, become resentful, throw in the towel and walk away, saying, "I didn't want to play on this team anyway" or "The coach doesn't like me" or "They never gave me a fair chance." Others don't quit the team overtly, but they give up inside. They lose their spirit. They stay on the team but feel unimportant, uninvolved, disillusioned, disappointed, and sometimes disgruntled.

Not too long ago in California, the sports page in Los Angeles carried an interesting headline about their local professional basketball team, which read, "Lakers Land Major Star and Second Stringer." A minister in the vicinity picked up that headline and preached a sermon on the subject, titled "When You're Not Number One." The question he asked was, "How would you react to being called a 'second stringer'?" What about your wife or son saying, "That's my husband or my dad. He's second string"?

How do we respond to being a "scrub," a "reserve," a "sub"? Can we accept that role willingly or with grace? What does God expect from second stringers? Well, as a matter of fact, Jesus told a parable once that speaks to this. It was the story about three men to whom an employer entrusted his business affairs. The employer gave five talents to one servant, two talents to another, and to the third man, he gave one talent. Notice the Scripture points out that he gave to each of them according to their abilities, and then the employer went away. Of course you recall from the story that the first two men doubled their portions and were congratulated, but the third man was rebuked because he was afraid and so he had hidden his one talent in the ground.

Now, normally at this point, we go off in the direction of the one-talent servant, as we consider how and why he failed. But one fellow in this parable of the talents has received far too little attention: the middle man, the man with the two talents; yes, the second stringer. Strange, isn't it, that we never talk about him. Yet we are really more akin to this middle man—and there is so much to learn from him, especially for those moments in life when we find ourselves on the backup squad or in the reserve role or in the substitute position.

From his response to his challenge in the story, we learn in a subtle way what God expects from us when we have to play second string. Let's look at this together.

First, the Two-Talent Servant Reminds Us That God Expects Us to Be the Best We Can Be

We don't have to be Moses. We don't have to be Paul. We don't have to be Luther, Wesley, or Saint Francis or Mother Teresa. We don't have to be the best there ever was. We don't have to be the best there ever will be. We don't have to be the five-talent servant; God doesn't expect that of us. God only expects us to be the best we can be, to discover our uniqueness, our specialness, to seize it and celebrate it.

Remember that poignant line in Arthur Miller's play *Death of a Salesman.* Willy Loman had died, and someone says of him: "He never knew who he was."

This is one of the quiet tragedies of life. Many people go through life never knowing who they are, never finding their specialness, trying to be something they are not, trying to be a five-talent servant when, for the life of them, all they have is two talents or three, or maybe even only one.

Martin Buber once told the story of a rabbi who, on his deathbed, sees himself as a loser. The rabbi laments that in the world to come, he will not be asked why he wasn't Moses; rather, he will be asked why he wasn't himself.

Whether we are a second stringer or a third stringer, whether we have two talents or three or one, doesn't really matter. All that matters is that we do the best we can do, that we be the best we can be, that we find our unique specialness and claim it and enjoy it and use it productively.

Douglas Malloch once wrote a poem that encourages us to be the best we can possibly be titled, "Be the Best of Whatever You Are." He indicates in the poem that we can't all be the biggest tree at the top of the hill, but we can strive to be the best of whatever we are, whether it be a scrub or a bush or a plant or a flower in the valley. "Be a bush if you can't be a tree," he says, but be the best bush you can possibly be. He goes on to point out that we can't all be the biggest fish in the lake; we can't all be the captain of the ship, but wherever life takes us, we can try to be the very best of whatever we are.

God only expects us to do our best; not somebody else's best, just our best. The two-talent servant reminds us of that.

Second, the Two-Talent Servant Reminds Us That God Expects Us to Use Our Talents to the Fullest

Recently, I read in a magazine about a college student who, on his first day on campus, was asked to write a theme on the story of his life. A few days later, the professor returned the student's paper graded C+. The student was irate about his grade and protested immediately. "What right," he demanded, "do you have to rate my life a C+?"

Now, I'm sure the professor had other things in mind when he gave that student his grade. But the truth is that many people do indeed have C+ lives.

Remember the old story about the man who went to a psychiatrist and complained that he had an inferiority complex. The psychiatrist tested him and announced, "Well, I have good news and bad news for you. The good news is that you *don't* have a complex; the bad news is that you *are* inferior!"

All of us feel inferior at times. But it helps to remember this: it isn't what we have, but the way we use what we have that makes life count.

Don't miss this point in Jesus' parable of the talents: When the two-talent servant used what he had, even though it was limited, even though it was less than another, his satisfaction from the fulfilled trust was equal to the reward received by the one who got far more in the beginning.

The point is that you can gain as much joy using to the fullest what you have as the fellow who has everything gains from using his. Let me illustrate that.

In the Olympics when the athletes take the awards stand and receive their medals, they are filled with joy and pride over what they have worked for and accomplished as the greatest athletes in the world but, let me ask you something, have you ever seen the Special Olympics, athletes with disabilities, of all ages, running and jumping and competing for all they are worth? Talk about joy and pride and accomplishment; look at the faces of those athletes. No joy could be greater, no pride could be greater because they are using their talents, challenged as they may be, to the fullest: and that's all God expects from any of his children.

G. A. Studdert-Kennedy once wrote a powerful and poignant poem that reminds us that it is the day in, day out commitment to God that really counts. He laments that sometimes we wish we could do one great deed and let that take care of everything, but the reality is that life doesn't work that way. This is not God's way or God's will. Rather, it is the way of daily discipleship. He puts it like this: We don't reach up to God by one grand or spectacular action, but instead it is "deed by deed and tear by tear, / Our souls must climb to thee."

Studdert-Kennedy only stated poetically what biblical writers declared long before, namely, if we can only serve in the small jobs, or in the remote corners or in the nitty-gritty areas, that's greatness in God's eyes—when we give our all. And there is joy and peace to be found even in those unlikely places of menial service. It's not what you have, but how you use what you have that brings peace and joy and fulfillment. God expects us to be the best we can be and to use our talents to the fullest. It's not how big your position is, it's not how big your talent is, it's only how big your heart is that matters.

Now, here is a third idea.

Third, the Two-Talent Servant Reminds Us That God Expects Us to Make Our Work Meaningful

Over the years, scholars have debated what is the most intense desire within human beings. Some have said it is the will to pleasure; others have said it is the will to power; others have said it is the will to happiness; still others have said it is the will to security. Viktor Frankl, coming out of the prison camp in World War II, said he believed it was the will to meaning; and I believe he's right. Nothing is more important than having a sense of meaning in what you do.

This idea is one I see often in people's kitchens, usually on some piece of art hanging over the sink. It's a prayer-poem that celebrates the sacredness of practical work like preparing meals and washing dishes. In essence the prayer admits to God that most of us will never be famous saints, but we can bring love and warmth and joy to our work in the kitchen with the pots and pans, and that all work that is dedicated to God is indeed sacred. The prayer-poem then ends with these words: "Accept this service that I do, I do it unto Thee."

"I do it unto Thee": this is indeed the key to meaning in our lives, to do everything we do as if God were our employer, to do everything we do as if we were doing it for God as his partner, as his coworker.

What does God expect of us? The parable makes it clear: God expects us to be the best we can be. He expects us to use our talents to the fullest, and he expects us to make our work meaningful and productive and creative by seeing our work as unto the Lord.

4

Vision
"The Parable of the Lighted Candle"

Scripture: Luke 11:33-36

Recently I asked a friend in the medical profession to give me a good definition of what a cataract is. The description of a cataract given to me by my friend was even better and more helpful than I expected it to be. Here's the definition, and as you read it, think with me about what might be spiritual cataracts for us.

"In medical terms a cataract is a clouding over of the lens of the eye. This filminess causes a loss of transparency and obstructs the passage of light into the eye thereby causing distorted vision. There is no pain; the loss of vision is gradual; it slips up on you. The cataract abnormality may occur in younger people as a result of some trauma, but most commonly occurs in adults. If left unattended, the cloudiness may become so heavy that no light can get through at all and vision is lost altogether. Cataracts can be removed by surgery."

This medical description brings to mind the words of Jesus in Luke 11 as he says, "Your eye is the lamp of your body. If your eye is healthy, your whole body is full of light; but if it is not healthy, your whole body will be full of darkness."

It is interesting to note here that in the Greek language (which was the original language of the New Testament), the word for *body* often meant more than the physical anatomy. Rather, it often meant what we in our modern-day world would call the total personality. With that in mind, let me paraphrase Jesus. The eye is the lamp of the total personality, or in other words, the way we see things, the way we look at things, the way we view things; the perspective we bring to things says a lot about us. The way we view other people says a lot about us and our spiritual lives. The way we view our job, material things, the world, and life says a lot about our spiritual health.

Remember that episode in the old *Andy Griffith Show* when Barney Fife, the nervous deputy of Mayberry, decides to become an amateur psychiatrist. He sends off for an amateur psychiatry kit. When it arrives, he tries it out on Otis, one of the town characters, using the classic ink blot test. Otis is in jail again for being inebriated in public. Barney shows Otis one of the ink blots and says, "Look at this, Otis, and tell me what you see!" Otis answers, "I see a bat!" Barney gets upset and says, "That's the difference between you and me, Otis. You see a bat and I see a butterfly!"

Well, for once in his life, Barney was precisely on target; the difference between people is indeed often most clearly demonstrated by the way we see things. The poet put it like this: "Two men looked out prison bars; one saw mud, the other saw stars."

When Jesus implies that we should beware of spiritual cataracts, he is reminding us that there are certain obvious things that can blind our eyes or cloud and distort our vision. What might those things be? That is the question this parable puts before us. What are the spiritual cataracts that can block out the light and "fuzzy up" our vision?

What comes to your mind? Well, here are a few spiritual cataracts I thought of and put down. I'm sure you will think of others, but for now, let's try these on for size.

First, There Is the Spiritual Cataract of Prejudice

Prejudice is a spiritual cataract. I don't know of anything that can distort our vision more than prejudice. It absolutely blinds us! Remember the story about the very boring, highly negative, extremely judgmental guest preacher who was invited to preach at the Yale University Chapel. He took the word *Yale* as his outline, and let each letter, Y-A-L-E, serve as a point of his sermon.

He said the Y stood for *youth* and he preached twenty boring, wearisome, negative, harsh minutes on the failings of today's youth. Then he said the letter A stood for *apathy*—and he preached twenty more judgmental, tiresome minutes about how apathetic young people are today. Next, he said the letter L stood for *laziness* and he droned on for another twenty minutes about how lazy young people are in our time. Finally, he came to the E in the word *Yale* (he had already preached for over an hour) and he said the E stood for *emptiness* and he railed on twenty more boring, negative, critical, judgmental, tedious minutes on the emptiness of modern-day young people.

Finally, finally, he was through. At the conclusion of the service, the choir and the guest preacher recessed down the center aisle. On the last row, the preacher saw a freshman student down on his knees praying fervently. The guest preacher was thrilled to see that his message had so touched and inspired this Yale student. The preacher stopped and asked the young man what he had said in his sermon that had so moved one freshman to such fervent prayer. The student answered, "I was just thanking God that I go to Yale and not to the Massachusetts Institute of Technology! That would have taken eleven hours and twenty minutes!"

Now, in my opinion, that preacher made three big mistakes that day. First, he preached too long. Second, he was too judgmental. The gospel is, after all, good news. But worst of all, he exposed his prejudice toward young people. Prejudice literally means to "pre-judge," and it's a terrible thing! To lump people into groups is blind and unfair and often very cruel. To think that all young people are alike, to think that all musicians are alike, to think that all women are alike, to think that all southerners or northerners are alike is wrong.

To lump all artists or all athletes or all people over the age of thirty into a group is unfair. To think that all teachers or all psychiatrists or all African Americans or all Hispanics or all Asians or all redheaded people are the same is blind and wrong. At best, it is narrow stereotyping. At worst, it is heartbreaking cruelty! Prejudice distorts the vision because it will not look at new facts. It is lazy and it in un-Christian. It blinds us to the uniqueness and individuality of each of God's children. Prejudice is a spiritual cataract that clouds our vision of other people.

Second, There Is the Spiritual Cataract of Narrowness

Narrowness, tunnel vision, closed-mindedness— whatever you want to call it—it is a spiritual cataract. Interestingly, my friend in the medical profession told me that one of the consequences of the cataract as it begins to grow on your eye is that you lose your peripheral vision—you can see only one way! That's what closed-mindedness is, the inability to see anybody else's way but yours.

There is an old story about a major league baseball manager who needed some help for his team as they were in the thick of a heated pennant race. He sent his best scout down to the minor leagues to find a good hitter. The next day the scout called back and he was so excited he could hardly speak. "I've found just the player we need," he said. "He's terrific! With this guy, we can win the World Series! It's unbelievable how good he is! He could come to the major leagues today and become an instant star! He is without question the best baseball player I have ever seen!" The manager said, "Can he hit?" "Well, no," answered the scout. "He's a pitcher. But he pitched a perfect game. Every pitch was in the strike zone. He didn't walk anybody. He struck out every hitter—a no-hitter, a perfect game! In fact, only one player on the other team touched the ball with the bat, and that was a foul tip!" The manager said, "Forget about the pitcher! Hire the guy who fouled one off. What we need is a hitter!"

Well, the point is clear—the narrow view blinds us to new possibilities. The manager had it in his mind that the only way to help his team was with a new hitter, and blinded by that narrow view, he missed the greatest player of all time! Narrowness is a spiritual cataract because it blinds us to new opportunities, new possibilities, new truths, and new ways.

Third, There Is the Spiritual Cataract of Jealousy

Have you ever heard the expression, "He is so jealous, he can't see straight"? That's pretty much on target. It fits. Resentment of others clouds our view. Envy distorts our vision. Jealousy does indeed blind us! Shakespeare knew about this. He wrote one of his most famous plays about it. Remember *Othello*? Othello loved Desdemona so much, and she loved him. But then Iago planted the seed of doubt in Othello's mind, the seed of jealousy. In the end, Othello smothered his beloved Desdemona to death with a pillow because his jealousy had driven him into a blind rage. That is what jealousy does to us, and Shakespeare was right in calling it a tragedy, because it is tragic when prejudice or narrowness or jealousy becomes a spiritual cataract.

There are many others we could mention—fear, despair, hate, selfishness. These, too, can distort our vision. Let me conclude with this. Remember how the text reads: "If your eye is healthy, your whole body is full of light; but if it is not healthy, your body is full of darkness." Or in other words, when we look at things with graciousness and generosity and love, our lives are full of joy and gratitude. But, when we look at everything with hostility and cynicism, we find ourselves likely prospects for a life of sadness, misery, and loneliness. If we want to have 20/20 vision spiritually, then the way to do it is to let the Great Physician come into our lives and perform surgery to take away everything in us that is grudging so that we can see everything and everybody with the eyes of generosity, the eyes of goodwill, the eyes of compassion, the eyes of love. The hymn writer said it beautifully:

> Open my eyes, that I may see
>   glimpses of truth thou hast for me;

Place in my hands the wonderful key
   that shall unclasp and set me free.
Silently now I wait for thee,
   ready, my God, thy will to see.
Open my eyes, illumine me,
    Spirit divine!

("Open My Eyes, That I May See,"
Clara H. Scott, 1895)

5

Listening

"God Speaks, and the Church Is Our Hearing Aid"

Scripture: Mark 4:1-9

A few years ago I flew to Nashville, Tennessee, to work with my publisher and a production company on a video project they were producing in connection with my book *Yes, Lord, I Have Sinned, but I Have Several Excellent Excuses*. We taped twelve video presentations to coincide with the twelve chapters of the book, so that Sunday school classes could see and hear me talking about my thoughts on the material in the book.

Now, I have been doing television for over thirty years, and in all that time I had never used any kind of makeup—until now!

They brought in a makeup artist who had done Sharon Stone's makeup for a movie she shot in Nashville, and the makeup artist put so much makeup on me that when I looked in the mirror, I thought I looked like I should be in a horror movie called *The Curse of the Walking Corpse*! My face was so made-up, so chalky, that I looked like a member of the Munster family!

Now, on the video my face looked OK (considering what they had to work with) but in real life, I felt as though I had on more makeup than Michael Jackson!

On the final afternoon of the taping, we finished at 4:00 p.m., and our dinner meeting time wasn't until 6:00 p.m. I had a two-hour window of time. I thought this would be a good time to return a couple of sportcoats to my brother, Bob. Bob and his wife live in Nashville. The production crew had wanted me to look different in each video presentation. After each segment, I would change shirts and ties and jackets. I had borrowed two sportcoats from my brother and I was anxious to return them safely to him before flying back to Houston the next day.

My brother told me that he would meet me halfway. He said, "Let's meet in the circle drive at Brentwood United Methodist Church in ten minutes." When I arrived, Bob was already there. I returned the sportcoats, and then we stood there and visited for a while.

Just then, a handsome young man came walking across the church's front lawn, and my brother said, "Do you know who that is?" No, I didn't. "Well, that's the youth minister here; you know his dad." His father and I had gone through college and through seminary together, and he had been a good friend over the years. So, Bob called the youth minister over so we could meet.

I told the youth minister how much I respected his dad, how we had gone through college and seminary together and that I knew his mother well too and that I remembered the day he was born. Now, the youth minister was listening to me intently, but he was looking at me in a very strange way. He just kept staring at me, studying me with a perplexed expression.

Just as we concluded our visit and the young man turned to walk away, it suddenly hit me; I realized why he had stared at me so strangely: it was the makeup!

I ran after him and said, "Let me explain why I have all this makeup on. It's because I just came from making some video presentations for my publisher, and they put this makeup on me for the taping." The youth minister said, "I am so glad you told me because I was drawing my own conclusions—and that was not one of them!"

Well, the point is clear: it is so easy to draw wrong conclusions if we don't have the truth. I want to share with you an important conclusion I have drawn about the church based on the truth of Christ, the truth of the Bible, the truth of church history, and the truth of my own personal experience.

That conclusion can be expressed like this: God is speaking to us, but we need a hearing aid to help us hear God's voice, and this is the role of the church. God speaks, and the church is our hearing aid.

In Mark 4, Jesus gives us the parable of the sower, the seed, and the soils. Many scholars believe that this parable is about the importance of listening.

Jesus actually says it like this: "Those who have ears to hear let them hear!" However, sometimes our natural ears are not enough. Three of the four different kinds of soils mentioned in this parable are not promising. The path soil represents the closed-minded listeners, the persons so hardened by life that they tune out, they stonewall, they refuse to listen to the point of view of anyone else. The rocky soil represents the excitable but shallow listeners. They listen superficially. They get excited at first, but it doesn't last because there is no depth of commitment, no deep roots. The thorny soil represents the listeners with mixed-up priorities. They give their energy and resources to the "thorns of life" and neglect the things that really matter. The fourth soil in the parable is the good soil. This good soil represents listeners who gracefully receive the seed of God's word and who work with it to bring forth new life and a great harvest.

But the fact that in Jesus' list of soils (listeners), three of the four are not receptive strongly underscores the fact that when it comes to listening well, we need help! We need a hearing aid, and this is where the church comes in.

In his last book, *A Spiritual Autobiography*, William Barclay wrote about his hearing problems and how he dealt with them. Here are his words:

> For many years, I have been stone deaf . . . and I want to say a word on hearing aids. Some people do not like to wear one because it makes them noticeable. Well, you are far more noticeable when you are deaf than when you are wearing a hearing aid, because for some strange reason people are full of sympathy for the blind, but find deaf people no better than a nuisance.
>
> Of course, I would like not to be deaf, but I have never found that being deaf stopped me doing anything that I wanted to do . . . because a very wonderful hearing aid has enabled me to overcome that handicap almost completely . . . so completely that until this year my main hobby was conducting choir. (William Barclay, *A Spiritual Autobiography* [Grand Rapids: William B. Eerdmans Publishing Co., 1975], 20–21)

All the way from the cumbersome, primitive ear trumpet to the attractive, modern electronic devices, hearing aids have been wonderfully helpful to those who need them.

In a way, this is precisely what the church does for us. The church is our hearing aid today! God speaks to us but we need assistance sometimes in hearing the message clearly. The church can help us tune in better.

Let me show you what I mean by being more specific with three thoughts about this. Are you ready? Here is number one.

First of All, God Speaks a Word of Calling to Us, and the Church Is Our Hearing Aid

God calls us to service, to mission, to ministry, and the church (when it is at its best) helps us hear God's call and respond. The church teaches us that God chooses to use us. He has a job for us. He wants to put us to work.

Let me illustrate that personally by telling you about my own call to the ministry and how the church helped me to hear it. When people think of the call to ministry, they often think of highly dramatic, even miraculous happenings like

- Moses before the burning bush
- Paul being blinded on the Damascus road

- Luther caught in a thunderstorm
- Wesley being saved from a burning house

But God didn't call me through a burning bush. He didn't blind me. He didn't call me in a storm or rescue me from a burning house.

Please don't misunderstand me! I am not disparaging dramatic calls. I am only saying that we can't limit God to acting only in that way. My call to the ministry took a gradual and unspectacular form.

It came in the church and through the church!

God spoke to me not just on one Sunday, but over many Sundays.

He spoke to me not just through one experience, but through many experiences.

He spoke to me not just through one person, but through many—Sunday school teachers, youth-group counselors, encouraging friends, members of my family, wonderful pastors, and one very unlikely person.

Her name was Marie. She was a town character who wore high-top tennis shoes and, year-round, a long red coat that was always buttoned to her chin.

She was very unusual, a strange personality, an "Apple Annie" type and a devoted member of our church. She was a most unlikely person for God to speak through and yet God spoke to me through her in this way.

I was in the tenth grade when suddenly one day after church Miss Marie approached me. It startled me a bit because I was a little afraid of her. She was a strange-looking character. "Jim, you don't know it yet," she said to me, "but God's gonna make a preacher out of you!" With that, she turned and walked away.

That haunted me for two years. I wondered why she would say something like that. I thought about it. *Was she right? Could that be possible?* I honestly didn't know. I prayed about it. I tested God. I asked for a sign, a visible, sensational, dramatic sign. And I got absolutely nothing! I asked for lightning; nothing! I asked for a sign in the clouds; nothing! I asked for it to rain; nothing! I asked for it to stop raining; it rained harder!

Then it dawned on me through the help of my pastor that the fact that I kept asking (that I wanted it so much) was God's way of calling me. I was looking out there somewhere, and God was calling me in here all along. The Apostle Paul once said, "My call is from God, not man" (Galatians 1:12, paraphrased). I would say, "My call is from God but the church (along with a very unlikely character named Miss Marie) was my hearing aid!"

Two quick comments here. First, to young people, let me just say that God is calling you to serve him and he may well be calling you to the ministry.

Second, to the church, my personal experience suggests something very important to us: that we should work at creating the warm kind of atmosphere whereby people can hear the voice of God.

Second, God Speaks a Word of Love to Us, and the Church Is Our Hearing Aid

Let me ask you something. What was the very first verse of Scripture you learned as a child in Sunday school? Do you remember? I do: "God is love"! I could hardly speak and already the church was teaching me that God is love.

Do you remember the first song you learned as a child in Sunday school? I do: "Jesus Loves Me"! And the second was "Praise Him! Praise Him! All the little children. God is love! God is love!" That's the good news of our faith, isn't it?

I once conducted the funeral of a lovely young woman. She was twenty-three years old when she died. She had battled leukemia for a little over two years and most of that time she was in the hospital. Toward the end, she had great trouble sleeping. Emotionally depleted, worn out, physically weak, and sometimes in great pain, she was heard singing in the middle of the night by her parents. Unable to sleep, she would sing quietly, peacefully, and confidently these words:

> Jesus loves me! This I know,
> For the Bible tells me so.
> Little ones to Him belong;
> They are weak, but He is strong.
> Yes, Jesus loves me!
> Yes, Jesus loves me!
> Yes, Jesus loves me!
> The Bible tells me so.

What better thing to remember at a time like that—that God is with us, that God loves us, that he is our strength and he will see us through, in this life and the next?

God loves us and the other side of that coin is that he wants us to be loving people. He wants us to imitate his loving ways.

This is the point of the parable of the prodigal son. In this parable, we see one who needs love (the prodigal), one who gives love (the father), and one who is unwilling to love (the elder brother). This great parable makes it dramatically clear that the father was right.

The church reminds us over and over again about God's gracious, loving ways, and how God wants us to be loving like him. Or, in other words, God speaks a word of calling to us and God speaks a word of love to us, and the church is our hearing aid.

Third and Finally, God Speaks a Word of Encouragement, and the Church Is Our Hearing Aid

Over the years, I have had people ask me, "What do you enjoy most about your work?" I love to preach and teach and would probably put those at the top of the list, but very close to the top I would put the ministry of encouragement. I believe with all my heart that people today need to hear from God and from the church a word of encouragement.

At a national coaches conference some years ago, a famous coach was the guest speaker. He spoke on the subject of how important it is to encourage one another. He told of a game back in the late 1970s.

Going into the season the team was confident. They had great talent, especially at quarterback, where the team had three players who were about equal.

Before the season, the second-string quarterback got hurt and was going to be out for the season. Coach felt sorry for the young man, but he thought, *We will be OK because we've got two more.*

However, in a game on a sunny Saturday afternoon, the first-string quarterback got badly hurt. Confidently, coach sent in the third-string quarterback—*after all*, he thought, *there is not much difference between the three quarterbacks in talent and experience.* But a few plays later, he too got injured in the game.

Coach didn't know what to do. The fourth-string quarterback was a senior; in four years he had never been in a game, not one play, but the coach had no other choice, so he called for him.

Meanwhile, out on field, the team's all-star running back had gathered the other ten players into a huddle, and he said to them: "Fellows, we are in big trouble here. I don't know who Coach is going to send in. But, whoever it is, we have got to make him feel like he is the best quarterback in America. We have got to make him feel like he is the man of the hour and this is his moment. We have got to make him feel like we believe in him, we trust him, and we know he can do it!"

So, when that fourth-string senior quarterback (who had never played a down) started onto the field, there was fear in his eyes, but it didn't last long. The offensive team ran to meet him. They hugged him. They patted him on the back. They told him they were ready and that they believed in him. They pumped him up so much that they not only won that game but all the rest and they won the conference championship with an 11-0 record!

There we see it: the power of encouragement. We in the church should be first and foremost the sons and daughters of encouragement.

And as Christians we have a lot to be encouraged about. The point of the parable of the sower in Mark 4 is wrapped up in encouragement, because in the end, against all odds, there was a great harvest. So, the lesson is this: be faithful, broadcast the seed of God's word, and God in the end will bring a great harvest!

The church is our hearing aid, enabling us to hear God's amazing words of calling, love, and encouragement, and this underscores for us just how important, how essential, how crucial the church is in our own lives, in our community, and in our world.

6

Action

"Use It or Lose It"

Scripture: Matthew 25:14-29

Recently I ran across a fascinating list of unusual answers given by children on some of their tests in school. In answer to the question "When was our nation founded?" one little boy wrote, "I didn't even know it was losted!" Another child said that "Socrates died from an overdose of wedlock." Asked to describe the famous painting of Whistler's mother, one student explained, "It shows a nice little lady sitting in a chair waiting for the repairman to bring back her TV set." Some more interesting statements included:

"A horse divided against itself cannot stand."

"The death of Thomas Jefferson was a big turning point in his life."

"Zanzibar is noted for its monkeys; the British governor lives there."

And here is my favorite. A little girl was asked to define the word *people*: "People are composed of girls and boys and men and women. Boys are no good until they are grown up and married. My mother is a woman, which is a grown-up girl with children. My father is so nice and I think he must have been a girl when he was a boy!"

Now, give the children an "E" for effort. They are trying to get at the truth. I want to try to get at the truth of one of the strangest verses in all of the Bible. The scripture from Matthew 25:29 at first glance may be confusing. Some people would list this as one of the most perplexing verses in the Bible: "For to all those who have, more will be given, and they will have an abundance; but from those who have nothing, even what they have will be taken away."

What does this mean? Why give more to the one who has plenty and take away from the one who has so little? It sounds so unfair, and for that reason the verse is a frustrating mystery to many people. To unravel the mystery, it helps to see the verse in context. It comes at the end of Jesus' parable of the talents. Jesus said a man was going on a journey. Before leaving, he called in three of his servants. The man left five talents with one servant. He left two talents with another servant, and he entrusted one talent to still another servant, and then he went away. During the man's absence, the servant with five talents traded with his and made five more; the servant with two talents used his to earn two more; but the servant with one talent buried his in the ground for safekeeping because he was afraid. He was afraid of his master, afraid of failure, afraid to take a risk, afraid to try, and so, paralyzed by his fear, he did nothing. He buried his talent in the ground.

When the master returned, he commended the two servants who had used their gifts and increased them. But when the one-talent servant came in for the accounting, the master became quite upset with him because he had done nothing. The master rebuked him, calling him "wicked" and "slothful." But more than that, the master took away the servant's one talent and gave it to the servant with ten talents. Then comes that haunting verse: "For to all those who have, more will be given, and they will have an abundance; but from those who have nothing, even what they have will be taken away."

What is this all about? The key is to understand that the true meaning stands out when we see that Jesus is not talking about money. He is not talking about bank stocks or real estate; rather, he is talking about our abilities, our talents, our capabilities, our gifts, and our inner determination to use what we have.

Jesus is underscoring a fascinating and dependable principle of life, namely, that if we don't use our gifts and talents, we lose them. If we don't use our abilities, they shrivel and die. The truth of that principle is as wide as life itself. Ask any athlete or musician, ask any artist or scholar, ask any salesperson or surgeon, any writer or preacher. Each in his or her own way will tell you from personal experience that it is true: Either we use our talents or we lose them. This principle literally pervades every area of life.

The Physical Level

We all know that it is true on the physical level. Our physical talents and capabilities and gifts are enhanced, improved, and increased by use, exercise, and practice. This is what gives the sailor her keen eye, the pianist his nimble wrist, the surgeon her deft hand, and the runner his grace and endurance.

Jesus is so right: the one who has the will and determination to exercise and use his talents physically increases them. We can also see in the physical world the other side of the coin: if we don't use our abilities, we lose them. For example, the mole that lives underground and the fish that swim in Echo River in Mammoth Cave have eyes, but they cannot see. They have neglected to use what they have, and nature has taken its natural revenge. The underground mole and the Mammoth Cave fish have eyes that outwardly are perfect, but inwardly the optic nerve is dead, killed by lack of use. Whether you are dealing with fish or moles or people, the principle holds true: either use it or you lose it.

Some years ago, professional golfer Byron Nelson was winning all the major golf tournaments. He played with such perfect precision that he was called the "Mechanical Man of the Fairways." But then he retired from the pro tour and came to live on his ranch in Texas. On the few occasions later when he emerged from his retirement to play again, he simply was no match for the leaders. He had proved long ago and many times over that he had the talent by winning so regularly on the tour; but when he stopped, he lost the competitive edge, he lost the power to win. This principle is dramatically true on the physical level. If we use our talents, we enhance them.

Happy Chandler was the governor of Kentucky for many years. He was asked late in his life what was the key to his long life and good health. He gave an interesting answer: "Early on in our marriage, my wife and I made an agreement. We decided that every time I got upset with her, that rather than argue, I would walk around the back yard in the open air until I calmed down." The questioner asked, "How did that help?" Happy Chandler, with a twinkle in his eye, responded, "Forty-five years of exercise in the open air can make you real healthy!"

Some years ago I was a pretty good athlete. I made the All-Memphis team twice in basketball.

All-District, Memphis Regional, I was mentioned on some of the all-state teams in Tennessee. I averaged twenty-two points a game my senior year in high school and went to college on an athletic work scholarship. But a few years ago I embarrassed myself silly in a basketball game.

It was United Methodist Day on the Centenary College campus. Children's choirs sang, the bishop was presented with a special gift from the college, and a group of ministers were asked to play a fifteen-minute basketball game during halftime of the Centenary-SMU game. I played, and this is what happened: my mind said, "Intercept that pass. Dribble full speed down the court. Fake out the defender. Dribble behind your back and soar high for a crowd-pleasing, double-pump, swooping reverse left-hand layup." That's what my mind said to my body.

My body answered back: "Who? Me?"

My mind said, "Yes, you. You can do it. You've done it before, and you can do it now. Go to it." That's what my mind said to my body.

My body answered back, "You gotta be kiddin'!"

My body refused to respond because it hadn't been used that way in so long. I hadn't exercised, I hadn't practiced, I hadn't played, and it was awful. I did pretty well for about thirty seconds, and after that it was terrible! I was the third-most embarrassed person in that arena: the two most embarrassed were our children, who kept saying repeatedly to their mother, "Just think, after this is over, he's actually gonna come over here and sit down beside us." I learned the hard way that Saturday afternoon the agonizing truth of this principle: if you don't use it, you lose it.

The Intellectual Level

It's also true on the intellectual level. If we work at it, if we stretch our minds, they grow, but if we put our minds into neutral and stop learning, our minds shrivel up on us.

We tend to think that some people are smart and others are not. The truth is that the difference is not so much in wisdom or brain capacity as it is in hard work. The good students are not just those who are smart. They are the ones who work at it, the ones willing to pay the price.

Longfellow expressed it well:

> The heights by great men reached and kept
> Were not attained by sudden flight,
> But they while their companions slept
> Were toiling upward in the night.

Hard work does it.

In the British Museum in London are displayed the original pages used by Thomas Gray in writing his now famous poem, "Elegy Written in a Country Churchyard." Displayed there are seventy-five drafts of that one poem. He wrote it, didn't quite like it, wrote it a second time; still not quite right, rewrote it and rewrote it seventy-five times before he got it into the form we now read.

Some years ago, a young boy came from a poor farm in Canada to America to become a minister. He never went to seminary; he couldn't afford it. He took a church in Baileyton, Tennessee. After a short time there, he went to pastor a church in St. Petersburg, Florida. The day he arrived, the church had 46 members and an average attendance of 34. The first Sunday's offering was $5.76. When the minister died forty years later, he was still serving the same church, but the membership was close to 4,000, and the average congregation each Sunday was over 2,500. He was known and respected as one of the finest preaching voices of our time and the author of several top-selling books. How could this be? How did J. Wallace Hamilton do it?

Bishop Gerald Kennedy answered, "How did he do it? What did it? Work. Hard work. He kept studying, stretching his mind, trying to improve. First of all, and beyond everything else, hard work did it for him."

Physically it is true, and intellectually it is true: either we use it or we lose it.

The Social Level

It's also true on the social level. If we learn how to interact with people, we can do pretty well, but if we go into seclusion and shut people out of our lives, we can get into trouble.

Linda is a friend of mine. She was in high school, a member of our church, and an active leader in our youth group. She was bright, outgoing, attractive, popular, and she loved people. When Linda finished college, she began to struggle with the call to the ministry. She thought God might be calling her into the ministry, but she wasn't sure. Since she had saved quite a bit of money and didn't have to work, she decided to go into seclusion for one year, to study and pray and meditate and listen for God's call. She wanted to separate herself from any outside distractions, so she refused to use the telephone. She would not answer the door; she didn't go out of her house; she would not see anybody. All she did was study. No television, no radio, no newspapers, no contact with the outside world.

Several months into the experiment her mother called me and asked me to go with her to Linda's home. She said, "Something has happened to Linda. This secluded lifestyle has changed her. She needs help. You'll have to see it to believe it."

We went together to Linda's home. I couldn't believe my eyes. When Linda heard us coming she was terrified. She ran to the back of the house to hide from us. She was hiding behind the drapes, peeping out fearfully with a panicked look on her face, scared to death to face another human being. It was obvious what she needed. She needed to get back into the world, back into society, and I'm happy to report she is now doing well. But the point is clear: it's true socially, as well as physically and intellectually: we use it or we lose it.

The Spiritual Level

If it's true that practice makes perfect in music, golf, art, poetry, speaking, writing, even relating to others, it must be true that practice enhances the spiritual graces. If you want to have a good prayer life, there is only one way to do it: you just pray, pray, and pray some more. You have to work at it.

If you want to have a good grasp of the Bible, there is only one way. You study the Scriptures—study, study, and study some more. Then read the dictionaries and commentaries and everything you can get your hands on about the Bible. That is the only way to do it.

If you want to be a good servant of the church, how do you do it? You get in the stream of the church and you go every time the doors of the church open. You get involved and participate; you go expectantly, hoping, learning it, and living it.

How do you become a good Christian? You live

it every day. You practice living the Christian life until you get it right. Either we live the faith or we lose it. Every time we say no to God, the longer we put him off, the more difficult it becomes to say yes to him. And the more we say yes to God, the *easier* it becomes to say yes to him and to life.

That's the choice that is open to us, spiritually, in our faith experience. We use it or we lose it.

STUDY GUIDE
SUGGESTIONS FOR LEADING A STUDY OF
Jesus' Parables About Discipleship

JOHN D. SCHROEDER

This book by James W. Moore examines some of Jesus' parables to see what we can learn from them about the characteristics of discipleship. To assist you in facilitating a discussion group, this study guide was created to help make this experience beneficial for both you and members of your group. Here are some thoughts on how you can help your group:

1. Distribute the book to participants before your first meeting and request that they come having read the first chapter. You may want to limit the size of your group to increase participation.

2. Begin your sessions on time. Your participants will appreciate your promptness. You

may wish to begin your first session with introductions and a brief get-acquainted time. Start each session by reading aloud the snapshot summary of the chapter for the day.

3. Select discussion questions and activities in advance. Note that the first question is a general question designed to get discussion going. The last question is designed to summarize the discussion. Feel free to change the order of the listed questions and to create your own questions. Allow a set amount of time for the questions and activities.

4. Remind participants that all questions are valid as part of the learning process. Encourage their participation in discussion by saying there are no wrong answers and that all input will be appreciated. Invite participants to share their thoughts, personal stories, and ideas as their comfort level allows.

5. Some questions may be more difficult to answer than others. If you ask a question and no one responds, begin the discussion by venturing an answer yourself. Then ask for com-

ments and other answers. Remember that some questions may have multiple answers.

6. Ask the question "Why?" or "Why do you believe that?" to help continue a discussion and give it greater depth.

7. Give everyone a chance to talk. Keep the conversation moving. Occasionally you may want to direct a question to a specific person who has been quiet. "Do you have anything to add?" is a good follow-up question to ask another person. If the topic of conversation gets off track, move ahead by asking the next question in your study guide.

8. Before moving from questions to activities, ask group members if they have any questions that have not been answered. Remember that as a leader, you do not have to know all the answers. Some answers may come from group members. Other answers may even need a bit of research. Your job is to keep the discussion moving and to encourage participation.

9. Review the activity in advance. Feel free to modify it or to create your own activity. Encourage participants to try the "at home" activity.

10. Following the conclusion of the activity, close with a brief prayer, praying either the printed prayer from the study guide or a prayer of your own. If your group desires, pause for individual prayer petitions.

11. Be grateful and supportive. Thank group members for their ideas and participation.

12. You are not expected to be a "perfect" leader. Just do the best you can by focusing on the participants and the lesson. God will help you lead this group.

13. Enjoy your time together!

SUGGESTIONS FOR PARTICIPANTS

1. What you will receive from this study will be in direct proportion to your involvement. Be an active participant!

2. Please make it a point to attend all sessions and to arrive on time so that you can receive the greatest benefit.

3. Read the chapter and review the study-guide questions prior to the meeting. You may want to jot down questions you have from the read-

ing and also answers to some of the study-guide questions.

4. Be supportive and appreciative of your group leader as well as the other members of your group. You are on a journey together.

5. Your participation is encouraged. Feel free to share your thoughts about the material being discussed.

6. Pray for your group and your leader.

Chapter 1
Unconditional Love: "What Is the Good News?"

SNAPSHOT SUMMARY

This chapter explores the parable of the prodigal son and shows how God is like a forgiving, loving parent, an example of unconditional love.

REFLECTION / DISCUSSION QUESTIONS

1. In your own words, what does *discipleship* mean? What are the benefits of examining Jesus' parables about discipleship together as a small group?
2. Recall a time when you were the recipient of unconditional love. Share the circumstances, and how it made you feel.
3. Why did Jesus tell the parable of the prodigal son? According to the author, what was Jesus' key message in it?
4. What can we learn about God from reading this parable?
5. Share a time when your patience was rewarded.

6. What lessons have you learned about forgiveness in recent years?

7. How is unconditional love different from other types of love? Is it difficult to love someone unconditionally? Why or why not?

8. Why did the elder son in the parable react as he did? In what ways are many of us like him?

9. Give some reasons why the parable of the prodigal son has been called the greatest story of all time.

10. How did your reading and discussion of this chapter personally enrich you? What additional insights or questions would you like to explore?

ACTIVITIES

As a group: Is there a recipe for unconditional love? Together, list some of the ingredients or elements of unconditional love. Start with a group definition of the term, then look at what is it that makes love unconditional.

At home: Reflect upon the parable of the prodigal son and its messages of patience, forgiveness, and unconditional love.

Prayer: *Dear God, thank you for loving us uncon-ditionally. You are a forgiving and loving parent to us. Help us show unconditional love to others. Amen.*

Chapter 2
Humility: "Presumptuous Religion"

SNAPSHOT SUMMARY

This chapter offers examples and warnings of the dangers of being presumptuous, and it encourages humility—the opposite of presumptuous religion.

REFLECTION / DISCUSSION QUESTIONS

1. Share a past encounter with a presumptuous person.
2. What causes people to be presumptuous? Why is it easy to fall into that trap?
3. Why did Jesus tell this parable of the wedding banquet and the seating arrangement of the guests? What truths was Jesus trying to get across?
4. Is it hard to be humble? Why or why not?

5. How does a person increase humility and decrease presumptuousness?
6. What makes presumptions so dangerous?
7. Reflect on / discuss possible warning signs that a person is arrogant or closed-minded.
8. How did Jesus demonstrate what it means to have a humble spirit?
9. List some of the different ways in which humility can be expressed.
10. How did your reading and discussion of this chapter personally enrich you? What additional insights or questions would you like to explore?

ACTIVITIES

As a group: Search your Bibles for examples of acts of humility. Share your findings with one another.

At home: Examine yourself for signs of presumptuous arrogance. Pray, asking God to guide your way.

Prayer: *Dear God, thank you for showing us what it means to have humility and to practice a humble faith. Keep us aware of the dangers of being a presumptuous person. Help us be open-minded and love others. Amen.*

Chapter 3
Service: "You Want Me to Play Second String?"

SNAPSHOT SUMMARY

This chapter uses Jesus' parable of the talents to remind us that God expects us to be the best we can be, to use our talents to the fullest, and to make our work meaningful.

REFLECTION / DISCUSSION QUESTIONS

1. Share a time when you were a "second stringer" or worked out of the spotlight.
2. What lessons can be found in the parable of the talents?
3. What sorts of conditions do people sometimes impose on their service to God or others?
4. How did Jesus demonstrate service to others? What can we learn from him?
5. God expects us to be the best we can be.

Elaborate on this idea and give an example of making your best effort.

6. Reflect on / discuss what it means to use your talents to the fullest.

7. Why are second-string players important in God's world?

8. How do you make work meaningful? Share your thoughts and ideas on this.

9. What are some of the keys to being a successful second stringer?

10. How did your reading and discussion of this chapter personally enrich you? What additional insights or questions would you like to explore?

ACTIVITIES

As a group: Use your Bibles to locate and identify some "second stringers" who served God. Talk about these people and what made them noteworthy or unique.

At home: Take an inventory of your talents and how you are using them to serve others. Are you a successful, selfless "team player" for God?

Prayer: *Dear God, thank you for the many opportunities you give us to minister to others. Help us do our best and make the best use of our talents. Remind us that we are working for you. Amen.*

Chapter 4
Vision: "The Parable of the Lighted Candle"

SNAPSHOT SUMMARY

This chapter explores spiritual cataracts such as prejudice, narrowness, and jealousy, which hinder our vision and prevent us from being a light to others.

REFLECTION / DISCUSSION QUESTIONS

1. What are spiritual cataracts, and how do you get them?
2. Share a time when you became aware that you had a spiritual cataract.
3. What important point was Jesus making in Luke 11:33-36? How does the message of this parable apply to us today?

4. How does our vision—the way we see things—influence our spiritual life and health?

5. In what ways does prejudice cloud our spiritual vision? Why is prejudice dangerous? How can it harm us and others?

6. Give some reasons why people are prejudiced and name some common prejudices.

7. Share a time when you realized you were being closed-minded.

8. In what ways does narrowness blind us? How is it different from or similar to prejudice?

9. List some common cures for prejudice, narrowness, and jealousy.

10. How did your reading and discussion of this chapter personally enrich you? What additional insights or questions would you like to explore?

ACTIVITIES

As a group: Create a "Vision Test for Christians." Make a list of things that Christians should be able to see, such as the good in others, people suffering, those who are hungry, and so on. Give each member of your group an opportunity to contribute ideas to the list.

At home: Give yourself a "vision checkup," to see if you have spiritual cataracts. Look for symptoms of prejudice, narrowness, and jealousy. If you think you have a problem, ask God to provide you with guidance in finding a spiritual cure.

Prayer: *Dear God, thank you for reminding us of spiritual diseases that hinder our ministry. Help us see clearly so that we can help others in need and do your will. Amen.*

Chapter 5
Listening: "God Speaks, and the Church Is Our Hearing Aid"

SNAPSHOT SUMMARY

This chapter examines the parable of the sower and the soils to show how the church helps us hear God's call to service, God's love, and God's encouragement.

REFLECTION / DISCUSSION QUESTIONS

1. What qualities does a good listener possess?
2. Reflect on / discuss how the parable of the sower and the soils relates to listening.

3. When it comes to faith, why is good hearing important? What happens when your hearing is impaired?
4. Why do we need the church to assist us in spiritual hearing?
5. What often prevents people from hearing the word of God? List some of the obstacles.
6. Name some symptoms that indicate you may need a spiritual hearing aid.
7. Reflect on / discuss different ways in which God calls us to ministry.
8. Name some ways in which the church demonstrates God's love and also helps us hear and experience God's love.
9. How do you create a warm type of atmosphere where people can hear the voice of God? Share some of your ideas.
10. How did your reading and discussion of this chapter personally enrich you? What additional insights or questions would you like to explore?

ACTIVITIES

As a group: Create a list of ideas for how individual Christians can help make the church a more effective hearing aid. Or practice your spiritual listening skills: designate five minutes of quiet time where members can pray, meditate, reflect, and listen to God. After five minutes, ask members to share how they feel and what they experienced.

At home: Focus on listening this week. Make a special effort to listen to God as well as friends, family, and strangers. Remind yourself that listening can be a valuable ministry.

Prayer: *Dear God, thank you for giving us the church to better hear your calling, your love, and your encouragement. Remind us that we can all improve our listening skills and become more effective ministers. Amen.*

Chapter 6
Action: "Use It or Lose It"

SNAPSHOT SUMMARY

This chapter explores the principle that either we use our God-given talents or we lose them in the physical, intellectual, and social levels of our life.

REFLECTION / DISCUSSION QUESTIONS

1. Reread Matthew 25:29, and reflect on / discuss how its message applies to us today.
2. Name a talent or skill you possess that you would lose if you did not use it.
3. List some ways talents and gifts are lost through lack of use.
4. Reflect on / discuss some of the use-it-or-lose-it examples from the physical level of life.
5. What are some different ways to stretch the mind and to keep on learning?
6. Reflect on / discuss the idea that either we live our faith or we lose our faith.
7. What has helped you grow spiritually?
8. How does one become a good Christian?
9. Name some talents and skills that people can put to work at church.
10. How did your reading and discussion of this chapter personally enrich you? What additional insights or questions would you like to explore?

ACTIVITIES

As a group: Let each member write a brief prayer related to using his or her skills and talents. Add these prayers to the closing group prayer.

At home: Consider what you have gained from your reading and discussion of this book and from your small-group experience. What changes do you want to make in your life to be a better Christian?

Prayer: *Dear God, thank you for this opportunity to learn about discipleship through the parables of Jesus. Help us become better ministers to others and demonstrate Christ's love for all. Amen.*